The World's Best Irish Jokes

Mr "O'S"

The World's Best Irish Jokes

Illustrated by Peter Townsend

HarperCollins*Publishers*

HarperCollins*Publishers*
77–85 Fulham Palace Road,
Hammersmith, London W6 8JB

This paperback edition 1994
1 3 5 7 9 8 6 4 2

First published in Great Britain by
Angus & Robertson (UK) 1982
Reprinted twenty-three times

ISBN 0 00 638409 9

Set in Goudy Old Style Bold

Printed in Great Britain by
HarperCollinsManufacturing Glasgow

Introduction

I am emboldened to put together this modest collection which is mainly levelled against my countrymen by the very fact that many of these jokes were told me by fellow expatriates. My two favourites are in fact true stories — one told by a Northern Irishman and the other by a Southerner.

My Northern Irish friend tells of his last trip home to Belfast, where he was telling his parents about how the whole world was laughing at the Irish.

"Why?" asked his father in some perplexity.

"I suppose they think it's funny fighting over religion," my friend replied.

"But it's not about religion," replied his dad indignantly. "It's those bloody Catholics — they want to take over the whole of Ireland."

My friend from the South (I shall call him Paddy for the ease of the telling) contributed this marvellous Irish joke against himself. He was having a jar with some mates when it was his turn to shout again. At the bar he overheard a cheerful group telling Irish stories. Inebriated rather than incensed, Paddy thought he'd get his own back with the gamesmanship known as the Irish defence, which goes as follows:

Paddy: "How do yez get an Oirish girl pregnant?"
Cedric, an Englishman: "I don't know old chap. How *do* you get an Irish girl pregnant?"
Paddy: "And yez think the Oirish are stupid!"

So on his next shout, Paddy hustled up to them and said: "And tell me now, does any of you know how to get an *Irishman* pregnant?"

But possibly one of the best Irish stories belongs to a famous Irishman of another century. The great satirist Jonathan Swift not only ruthlessly satirised the English, he scourged his countrymen as well and finally bequeathed them a hospital for the housing of lunatics —

"to show with one satiric touch,
no nation wanted it so much."

How do you make an Irishman laugh on Monday?

Tell him a joke on Friday.

A ventriloquist is telling Irish jokes in a pub, when an irate Irishman stands up: "You're makin' out we're all dumb and stupid. I oughtta punch you in the nose."

"I'm sorry sir, I . . ."

"Not you," says the Irishman, "I'm talking to that little fella on your knee."

"**H**ey," said a new arrival in the pub, "I've got some great Irish jokes."

"Before you start," said the big bloke in the corner, "I'm warning you, I'm Irish."

"Don't worry," said the newcomer, "I'll tell them slowly."

" Irish crop duster !! "

Paddy and Mick shared first prize of £500,000 in the Irish Sweepstakes and were celebrating their winnings over a jar of stout.

"But Paddy, Oi've been thinking," said Mick with a worried frown, "what will we do with all them beggin' letters?"

"Shure," said Paddy, "we'll go on sending 'em out."

At the party they threw to celebrate, Paddy played his famous party trick. He extends his hands to an unsuspecting bystander and says: "Pick a thumb, any thumb at all."

When the bystander complies, the Irishman puts his hands behind his back for a moment, then holds out his clenched fist.

"Okay, now which hand is it in?"

It's revolutionary Paris, 1789, and three spies from across the channel are about to be guillotined.

"Do you want to be beheaded on your back or your front?" the executioner asked Smith. "On my back," said Smith. "I'm not afraid of death."

So Smith was laid on his back under the knife. The executioner pulled the lever. Schlick...and the knife jammed. Smith was reprieved because no man can be sentenced to death twice.

Hoskins was next. He too chose to face the knife. Again the blade jammed, and Hoskins was reprieved.

Murphy was third. "Back or front?" "If it's good enough for Smith and Hoskins, it's good enough for me," and so Murphy was laid on his back under the blade.

"Begorrah," he said. "Just a minute. I think I can see why it jams."

An airman had to bail out, and landed battered and bruised in a field just outside Belfast. A crowd had gathered round, and one of them said to the airman, "What happened?"

He said, "My parachute wouldn't open."

The Irishman said, "Ye should have known. Nothing opens here on a Sunday."

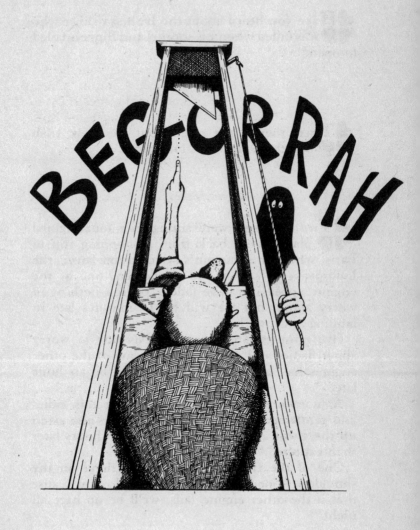

Have you heard about the Irish sky diver who was killed when his snorkel and flippers failed to open?

Then there's the one about the new Irish parachute. It opens on impact.

Two Irishmen were sitting in a four-engined plane flying back from a shopping trip to Paris when the captain's voice came over the loudspeaker. "Ladies and gentlemen, one of the engines appears to have failed. There's nothing to worry about, but we will be 15 minutes late in landing at Gatwick."

Five minutes later he said, "Nothing to worry about, ladies and gentlemen, but one of the other engines has failed, and we will now be an hour late."

A moment later, "Er...sorry about this ladies and gentlemen, but the third engine has also given up the ghost and we will now be two hours later than expected."

One of the Irishmen tapped his friend on the shoulder. "Good heavens, Patrick, do you realise that if the other engine fails, we'll be up here all night?"

The Aer Lingus plane was in trouble. "Mayday, Mayday," radioed the pilot.

"Cleared to land," came the answer from control. "Can you give us your height and position?"

"Well," said the pilot, "Oi'm five foot eight and Oi'm sittin' at the front of the plane."

But what about the Frenchman and the Irishman who both jumped off the Eiffel Tower?

The Frenchman got killed, and the Irishman got lost.

"'**T**is a terrible shame about that thick cloud," Mick complained to the two Americans who were standing nearby on the observation deck of the Empire State Building. "Yez can't see a thing."

"Well," one replied, "you may not be able to see bud, but it has its benefits. That there cloud is so thick that if you fell off here you'd hit the cloud and bounce right back again."

"Away with yez," said Mick. "Yez think because Oi'm Oirish Oi'm goin' to be believin' yez!"

"No, no," said the Yank. "It's true. Look, I'll prove it." So saying he jumped off the building. Two seconds later he hit the cloud and, sure enough, bounced back to the observation deck.

"Oi don't believe me oiyes," cried Mick.

"I'll do it again," said the Yank. "That cloud's as soft as a down pillow." Over the side he went and back up he came again.

"Well," said Mick, "seein's believin'. Oi'll have a go." Over the side jumped Mick. He hit the cloud and continued on through to be stopped forever by the pavement.

On the top of the tower the silent American turned to the other and said:

"You can be a real bastard at times, Superman!"

Paddy and Mick were at an air display, and there were planes doing all sorts of aerobatics. Paddy said to Mick, "I wouldn't like to be up there with one of those things."

Mick said, "An' I wouldn't like to be up there without one."

Pat was making his first aeroplane flight. The plane was up about 5,000 metres when the pilot sent it into a nose dive; it was headed straight for the city below. Pulling out of the dive, the pilot turned to Pat and laughed:

"I bet fifty per cent of those people down there thought we were falling," he said.

"Yes," said Pat, "and I'll bet fifty per cent of the people up here thought so too."

What do most of the people in Irish hospitals have in common?

They were all I.R.A. explosives experts.

The man in the hospital bed groaned and opened his eyes. His neighbour, in a kindly brogue, inquired:

"Would ye be feelin' orlright?"

"Where am I?"

"Hospital. D'ye want the good news or the bad news first?"

"Gimme the bad news — it can't be worse than how I feel!"

"Yez were in a smash — they had to operate — they've taken both yer feet off."

"What! Oh — gawd!"

"Yeah, Oi understand . . . so d'ye want the good news?"

"You must be joking —"

"No — the bloke in the next bed wants to buy yer shoes."

The Englishman explained to his doctor that all his life he'd really wanted to be an Irishman.

"Well," said the doctor, "there's an operation you can undergo. We just remove a portion of the brain and you'll be thinking and speaking like an Irishman in no time at all."

"Right," said the Englishman, "I'll have it."

Three weeks later the doctor walked into his patient's hospital room with a very worried expression on his face.

"I've made a terrible mistake," he explained. "I've removed eighty per cent of your brain instead of twenty per cent."

"She'll be right mate," drawled the patient with a grin.

On a recent Saturday night an ambulance went to collect a 'suspected overdose'. The patient was a very friendly Irish gentleman.

"Oi took 120 tablets last night," he said.

"You mean tonight," replied the ambulance man.

"No," said the patient, "Friday night."

"Today is Saturday and if you took them on Friday you'd be dead now," explained the driver.

"Oh well," said the patient, "it must have been Thursday, then."

Did you hear about the Irish newlyweds who sat up all night on their honeymoon waiting for their sexual relations to arrive?

The Irishwoman was elderly, but healthy and active; even so she insisted on a hysterectomy.
"But why?" asked the doctor.
"Sure," said the woman, "and me with 16 grandchildren already — I don't want any more."

Perhaps she'd heard about the Irish abortion clinic? It has a 12 month waiting list.

At an international medical symposium it was decided that some research should be devoted to the matter of the male penis with particular interest centring on why it was shaped with a knobbed end. Funds were set aside and three teaching hospitals were elected to investigate.

Royal Edinburgh was the first to report. In a 96 page document doctors distilled the results of tests conducted on over 6,000 subjects and questionnaires received from a further 4,000 respondents at a cost of £50,000. Their findings showed conclusively that the broader extremity of the member was to give additional pleasure to the male during sexual intercourse.

The Paris Hôpital du Sacré Coeur presented its findings soon after. Its report appeared at a cost of three million francs and its 74 pages outlined the positive responses from 5,000 countrymen. The French declared categorically that the glorious, retroussé shape of the penis gave added pleasure to the female partner during lovemaking.

St Patrick's, Dublin, was a little slower in presenting its report. Conducted on a sample of five at a cost of £5 it was nevertheless a serious document, one paragraph in length. "The knob at the end of the 'ould feller'," it concluded, "was to stop the hand from slipping off."

Patrick's wife lived way out in the country and took ill one day shortly before her child was due. It was quite dark when the doctor arrived, and he asked, "Where is the little lady, Patrick?"

"She's over there in the barn where she collapsed."

With Patrick holding the lamp the doctor set about his job.

"Patrick, you're the proud father of a little boy."

Patrick said, "Doctor, we'll have a drink."

"Just a minute. Hold the light a little closer. You're the father of two."

"We'll open a bottle," said Patrick.

"Wait," the doctor said. "Hold the light a little closer. You're the father of three."

"And sure it's going to be a celebration and all," said Patrick.

"Just a minute," said the doctor. "Hold the light a little closer."

"I don't want to be difficult, doctor," said Patrick, "but do you think this bloody light's attracting them?"

As he was passing the bend of a narrow but deep river in the heart of Warwickshire where he was on holiday, an Irishman named O'Cohen saw a man throw himself into the water. He dived in and pulled the man out. The stranger immediately thrust O'Cohen aside and threw himself back into the river. Unable to stand by and see a man commit suicide, O'Cohen went to the rescue again, and once more hauled the man out of the water. As soon as his saviour had turned his back, however, the would-be suicide hanged himself from a tree nearby.

At the inquest shortly afterwards the coroner demanded to know why O'Cohen had not cut the poor man down. "Shure," argued O'Cohen, "and Oi was after thinkin' the onfortunate character had pegged himself out to dry the same as meself."

Two Irishmen are on an iceberg.

Paddy says to Murphy, "We're saved, we're saved."

Murphy: "How do ye know that?"

Paddy: "Here comes the *Titanic*."

A famous operatic bass went to sing the part of Mephistopheles in "Faust" at a small theatre in the south of Ireland. He was very worried at the lack of scenery and effects, but noticed that the stage boasted a trap door such as is used by the demon king in pantomime to make his entrances and exits.

He decided to use it and arrived on the scene with a puff of smoke and a clap of thunder. Unfortunately there came an exit when the trap door stuck halfway, and there was the poor old devil, visible from the waist upwards, trying like mad to disappear into the nether regions by jumping on the trap. At that moment a boy in the gallery shouted out:

"Hurrah boys! Hell's full!"

Pat was a messenger in London, and was sent to the Bank of England on some business. The doorman said, "I'll hand you over to one of the clerks. He'll put you right."

The clerk came up and as he steered Pat inside, he said, "Is it for redemption, sir, or conversion?"

Pat said, "Am I in the right place? 'Tis the *Bank* of England I want. Not the *Church* of England."

"**D**on't jump," said Paddy to the man on the ledge. "Think of your wife and children."

"I've got no wife or children."

"Then think of your parents."

"I don't have any parents."

"Then think of St Patrick."

"Who's St Patrick?"

"Jump, ya bastard."

There's a good reason why Jesus was born in Jerusalem rather than Dublin. In Dublin they couldn't find three wise men or one virgin.

Two Irish friends greeted each other while waiting their turn at the bank window.

"This reminds me of Finnegan," remarked one.

"What about Finnegan?" inquired the other.

"'Tis a story that Finnegan died, and when he greeted St Peter, he said: 'It's a fine job you've had here for a long time.' 'Well, Finnegan,' said St Peter, 'here we count a million years as a minute and a million dollars as a cent.' 'Ah!' said Finnegan, 'I'm needing cash. Lend me a cent.' 'Sure,' said St Peter, 'just wait a minute.'"

There is a story about the Irishman who drowned while he was digging a grave for a friend. He'd wanted to be buried at sea.

During an Atlantic crossing the Jew and the Irishman had argued every day about the nature of eternal life. Shortly before the end of the voyage, the Jew fell ill, died, and was buried at sea with coal used to weight the body.

"Begorrah," said the Irishman, "Oi knew where he was bound for all the toime, but Oi niver dr'amed the h'athen would have to tote his own fuel!"

"**D**rink," said the Irish preacher, "is the greatest curse of the country. It makes yer quarrel with yer neighbours. It makes yer spend all yer rent money. It makes yer shoot at yer landlord — and it makes yer miss him."

Paddy was an inveterate drunkard. The priest met him one day, and gave him a strong lecture about drink.

He said, "If you continue drinking as you do, you'll gradually get smaller and smaller, and eventually you'll turn into a mouse."

This frightened the life out of Paddy. He went home that night, and said to his wife, "Bridget . . . if you should notice me getting smaller and smaller, will ye kill that blasted cat?"

There is the story of the Irish priest who was terribly mixed up. He went to see a psychiatrist who told him to forget his parish and his flock and go to London and enjoy himself for a few days. "Take your dog collar off and let your hair down," he said.

The priest did just that — he went to London . . . took off his dog collar . . . saw a movie . . . had a good meal and a drop of the hard stuff. Later that night, he found himself in Soho, in one of the 'clip joints'. He sat down at a table and a topless waitress came up and murmured: "What would you like to drink, Father?" He panicked, thought he must have left his collar on and stuttered: "How did you know I was a priest?"

"Oh! — I'm Sister Theresa. I go to the same psychiatrist!"

The Reverend Paisley was treating his parishioners to a grand old-fashioned 'hell-fire' sermon and repeated at frequent intervals, "There shall be weeping and gnashing of teeth."

Exasperated by this repetition, an aged member of the congregation shouted, "Let 'em gnash 'em as 'as 'em."

To which the preacher replied, "Madam, teeth will be provided."

The unwed Irish girl goes to confession: "Father, 'tis a shameful thing I have to confess. I'm pregnant."

"Are you sure it's yours?" asks the priest.

Cohen and Kelly were always arguing about religion.

One day Cohen said, "What are you putting your boy to?"

Kelly said, "I'll put him to the church."

Cohen said, "That's no life for a boy...no future."

Kelly said, "He might become a bishop."

Cohen said, "So! Living on charity."

Kelly still stuck to his point and said, "He could become the Pope."

Cohen said, "Living in a tomb in Rome? What life's that?"

Kelly got exasperated and said, "What would you expect the boy to be? Jesus Christ himself?"

Cohen gave a grin and said, "Well...one of our boys was."

Sean was confessing his sins to Father Patrick.

"Father, Oi've sinned. Oi've been beddin' with a married woman."

"Ye've what!" said the priest. "Carnal knowledge, God fergive ye, 'tis a mortal sin and Oi'll need to be knowing the name of the misbegotten sinner ye slept with."

"Shure, Oi couldn't tell ye that father. It wouldn't be honourable."

"Sean, ye let me be the judge o' that. Now who was it? — Was it Ada Murphy?"

"No," said Sean. "No it wasn't Ada Murphy, Father. Don't be askin' me, Oi can't say."

"Listen ye onfortunate divil. It will go better for ye if ye tell who it was. Was it Mary Finnegan?"

"No Father. It was not Mary Finnegan. Father forgive me but Oi cannot reveal who it was."

"Well if ye won't tell me, away and do penance," said the priest. "Say ten Hail Marys and three novenas."

Mick was waiting his turn outside the confessional. "How was it? What did you get?" he whispered to Sean.

"Foine," Sean whispered back. "Ten Hail Marys, three novenas and a couple of good leads."

Paddy was in America. He was patiently waiting, and watching the traffic cop on a busy street crossing.

The cop stopped the flow of traffic, and shouted, "Okay, pedestrians". Then he'd allow the traffic to pass. He'd done this several times, and Paddy still stood on the sidewalk.

After the cop had shouted "Pedestrians" for the tenth time, Paddy went over to him and said, "Is it not about toime ye let the Catholics across?"

A man walks out of a house in Belfast.

Another man walks up to him and sticks a gun to his head saying, "Are you a Protestant or a Catholic?"

The first man, not knowing how to reply for fear of being shot if he says the wrong thing, thinks for a minute and finally answers, "As a matter of fact, I'm Jewish."

At which the gunman chuckles, "Boy, I must be the luckiest Arab in Belfast tonight."

These two lads were in the army. One was Irish and the other was Jewish. They were doubling round the square, and when they had been halted, the Jewish boy, puffing, said to the Irish lad, "I hate doubling, Paddy."

The Irish lad said, "Oi'm not too keen on Tel Aviv, either."

A Rabbi and an Irish priest were alone together in the carriage of a train. After a while, the priest opened the conversation by saying, "I know that, in your religion, you are not supposed to eat pork...Have you actually ever tasted it?"

The Rabbi said, "I must tell the truth. Yes, I have, on the odd occasion."

Then the Rabbi had his turn of interrogation. He said, "Your religion too...I know you're supposed to be celibate. But..."

The priest said, "Yes, I know what you're going to ask. I have succumbed once or twice."

There was a silence for a while. Then the Rabbi peeped round the newspaper he was reading and said, "Better than pork, ain't it?"

Two Irishmen met in a pub and referred to the illness of a third.

"Poor Michael Hogan! Faith, I'm afraid he's going to die."

"And why would he die?" asked the other.

"Oh, he's got so thin. You're thin enough, and I'm thin — but by my soul, Michael Hogan is thinner than both of us put together."

" **P**addy," asked the barmaid. "What are those two bulges in the front of your trousers?"

"Ah," said Paddy. "They're hand grenades. Next time that queer O'Flaherty comes feeling my balls I'll blow his bloody fingers off."

A black, black night it was as Mick made his way homeward from the pub. Suddenly he heard a small voice crying for help and so, full of Guinness and good will to all men, he followed the sound till he came across the small figure of a leprechaun with his foot caught under a large stone. Mick freed the green-clad manikin, helped him gently to his feet and made sure all was well.

"Good sir," said the leprechaun, bowing stiffly and low, "I am in your debt and wish to repay yer kindness. I would deem it a favour if ye'd accept three fairy wishes."

"Shure now that would be foine," said Mick.

"Make a wish then," said the little man, "and whatever ye want, 'twill be granted."

"Oi wish Oi had a bottle of stout," said Mick.

No sooner were the words spoken than a bottle appeared in Mick's hand. Gently he unscrewed the top and supped the bottle.

"Sir," interrupted the leprechaun, "I don't mean to be rushing ye, but I must get on and ye still have two more wishes to make."

"Well," said Mick, "Oi wish this bottle would never be empty."

"Done," said the manikin.

Mick had another swig and another and, sure enough, after each the bottle would replenish itself.

"Glory be," said Mick, dancing a small jig and supping some more.

"And what's your third wish?" the leprechaun inquired politely.

"Shure now," said Mick, waving his magic bottle, "Oi'll have another one of these."

Two drunken Irishmen stumbled into a funeral parlour. They bumbled about until one fell over a piano. "Here's the coffin," he advised his mate.

"Do you recognise him?" asked the friend.

"No," admitted the first Irishman, "but he sure had a good set of teeth."

A cop pulls up two Irish drunks, and says to the first, "What's your name and address?"

"I'm Paddy O'Day, of no fixed address."

The cop turns to the second drunk and asks the same question. "I'm Seamus O'Toole, and I live in the flat above."

A policeman came across an inebriated gent late at night, going round and round a lamp post, tapping on it with his knuckles.

The cop said: "Now then. Come along. Get going..."

"Don't be daft, offisher," the drunk replied, "Oi'm walled in."

A big Irishman sauntered into a Dublin bar and shouted, "Which one of you is Michael O'Shea?"

A little man standing by the bar said, "That's me."

The big guy walked over to him and punched him in the mouth.

The little feller started laughing, so the big guy hit him again and he fell down, still laughing.

The hulk could not bear it. "Why are you still laughing after Oi've belted you?" he roared.

"The joke's on you," said the little man. "Oi'm not Michael O'Shea."

Paddy was strolling down a street, looking very disconsolate, and an English friend said, "What's the matter? You look browned off."

Paddy said, "Oi was in the pub over there, an' a fellow said the Oirish are always fighting and causin' trouble. Oi said they weren't."

The Englishman said, "What happened then?"

Paddy said, "Oi wrecked the place!"

An Irishman goes into a pub and the barman says, "Good evening, sir. What is your pleasure?"

"Thank you very much, Oi'll have a scotch and a box of matches, please."

He then puts five p on the counter and drinks the scotch.

"What's the five p for?"

The fellow says: "It's for the matches, Oi didn't really want a drink, but ye asked me so nicely what my pleasure was."

The barman begins to get cross. "Sir, I was only being polite."

The Irishman is adamant: "Oi'm sorry, but Oi refuse to pay."

He is barred from the pub.

Two weeks later he walks back in, and the barman shouts: "Hey you, out! I told you I never wanted to see you again."

The chap refuses. "You must have me mixed up with someone else. Oi've just come back after four months abroad."

After a close look the barman says: "I can't understand it; you must have a double."

"Thanks, and a box of matches as well, please."

There is the story of the two drunks who went one evening to look for the grave of a friend of theirs. They asked for Mulcahy of the Coombe and were told where he was buried. After traipsing about in the fog they found the grave, sure enough. One of the drunks spelt out the name: Terence Mulcahy. The other drunk was blinking up at a statue of Our Saviour the widow had got put up...and, after blinking up at the sacred figure, "Not a bloody bit like himself," says he. "That's not Mulcahy, whoever done it."

Mick had really had a skinful at the village pub one evening. When the pub closed, he went reeling down the village street, shaking hands with everyone. He finished up at the village pump, shaking hands with that.

After pumping the handle up and down for some time, he rolled over to another fellow and said, "Did ye see that? Father Riley shook me hand for about foive minutes...An' each time he shook it, he spat."

An Englishman walks into a country pub in the county of Galway.

"I say," he says, "how quaint! All this sawdust on the floor."

"Ah, that's not sawdust, Sor," says the barman, "that's last night's furniture."

An Irishman walked into a pub with a big, green bullfrog on his head.

"Where did you get that?" asked the barman.

The bullfrog replied, "Would you believe it started out as a wart on my behind?"

What's written on the bottom of an Irish whiskey bottle?

"Open other end."

What's written on the top of an Irish whiskey bottle?

"See other end for instructions."

This is a true story about Brendan Behan who one night collapsed in a diabetic coma in a Dublin street. It was at a time when he was at the height of his drunken notoriety and passers-by naturally thought he was dead drunk. They took him to the nearby surgery of one of Dublin's most fashionable and respected doctors. The doctor decided to take a cardiograph and, somewhat nervous of his patient, thought to humour him. He explained the workings of the cardiograph needle as it registered the faint heartbeats of the very sick and semiconscious Brendan.

"That needle there is writing down your pulses, Mr Behan, and I suppose, in its own way, it is probably the most important thing you have ever written!"

To which Behan replied: "Aye, and it's straight from me heart, too!"

O'Connell was staggering home with a pint of booze in his back pocket when he slipped and fell heavily. As he struggled to his feet he felt something wet running down his leg.

"Please God," he implored, "let it be blood."

How many Irishmen does it take to hit a nail into a wall? Twenty-two: one to hold the hammer, one to hold the nail, and 20 to shove the wall forward. Or . . .

At an Irish building site, a workman complained to the foreman: "These nails won't go into the wood."

"Of course not," said the foreman, "you're hammering them in head first. These nails are for the other side of the wall."

Another Irishman on a building site was going up and down the ladder, with the same hod of bricks each time.

One of his friends said, "What's the idea, Pat?"

He said, "Oi've had an argument with the foreman, an' Oi'm fooling him. He thinks I'm working."

How do you confuse an Irishman? Put three shovels in a corner and tell him to take his pick.

Patrick was a painter. One day, he was working away furiously, painting a door. One of the other painters said, "Take it easy, Pat. You'll have the union after you."

He said, "I've got to work fast. I want to finish this door before the paint runs out."

Irishman: "How am I going to measure the height of this ladder?"

Helpful bystander: "Lay it on its side and pace it out."

Irishman: "I want to measure its height, not its length."

How is an Irish ladder different from an ordinary one? It has a stop sign at the top.

Why is it that the windows on the bottom floors of Irish apartment buildings are always dirty?

They can't dig a hole deep enough to firm the ladder in.

When an Iranian oil rig caught fire recently, the Iranians thought first of calling Red Adair, the famous American firefighter. But not being on speaking terms with the Yanks, they had to settle for second best — Green Adair, the Irish expert.

Green agreed by phone to the commission at a fee of $50,000 and then took full details of the conflagration, the area it covered, the barrels it was estimated to consume per hour, the damage to derricks, etc. He'd be there in four hours, he promised.

The Iranians watched anxiously as Green's great green transport plane landed on the runway specially prepared near the rig. Almost as soon as the plane had touched down a great green fire engine shot out of its hatch and sped towards the fire.

The Iranians' anxiety turned to amazement as the fire engine plunged right into the centre of the fire and out jumped six green-clad figures who beat madly at the flames with old hessian potato sacks. For five hours they battled that fire with nothing between them and the engulfing flames but their hessian bags. And then, astonishingly, the fire was out.

As Green and his slightly singed helpers climbed back into the fire truck he was handed his cheque for $50,000.

"The first thing we do lads," Green whispered hoarsely, "is fix the brakes on the bloody truck."

One day two Irishmen were walking in the woods when they came across a sign saying "Tree Fellers Wanted". One of them said, "Ye know, Sean, it's a shame Paddy isn't with us today. We could have gotten the job."

Pat and Mick landed themselves a job at a sawmill. Just before morning tea Pat yelled: "Mick, I lost me finger."

"Have you now?" said Mick. "And how did you do it?"

"Oh, I just touched this big spinning thing here like thi...Damn. There goes another one."

The Irish attempt on Mount Everest was a valiant effort, but it failed: they ran out of scaffolding.

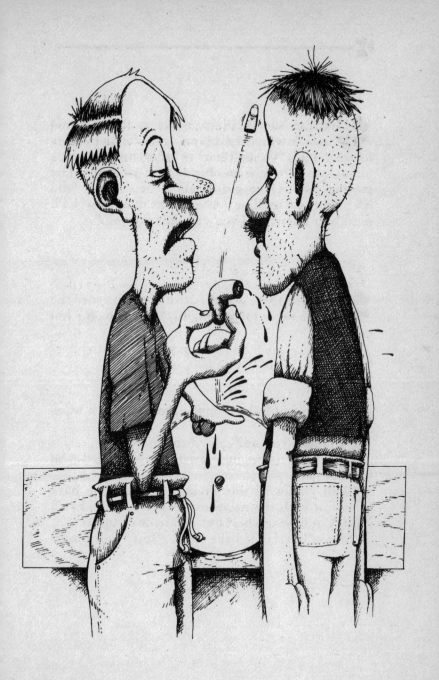

♣**B**rendan had applied at a factory for a job and was interviewed by an Irish foreman. The foreman said, "Oi can't start ye today, but if ye come tomorrow Oi might be able to give ye a job. The position is...Oi've got a fellow here today who hasn't turned up. If he doesn't come tomorrow, Oi'll send him home, and you can have his job."

♣**A**nd then there was the Irishman who sued the local baker for forging his signature on a hot cross bun.

♣**A** native of Ireland applied for a job in a warehouse.

"What can you do?" asked the foreman.

"Anything, sor, just anything," replied the hopeful man.

"Well," drawled the foreman, thinking to have some fun with the newcomer, "you seem to be all right. Could you wheel out a barrow of smoke?"

"Shure!" exclaimed the man. "Just fill it up for me!"

The Irishman at the front door said: "Morning, missus, Oi've come to mend your doorbell."

"I was expecting you yesterday," the woman replied.

"Shure now, but Oi rang then and got no answer."

And then there was the Irish gardener who broke his collar bone while raking up leaves — he fell out of the tree.

But not all Irishmen are dumb — after all, it was an Irishman who invented the helicopter ejection seat, an Irish surgeon who developed the appendix transplant and an Irishman who invented a solar-powered torch.

However it has not been all progress on the scientific front — they had to stop making iceblocks. The old lady who knew the recipe died.

Finnegan was the foreman on the railway, and was in the habit of sending very lengthy reports about minor incidents. He received a note from headquarters, telling him to be more brief and concise.

His next report couldn't have been more concise. It concerned an engine that had come off the rails.

His report read, "Off agin. On agin. Off agin. Finnegan."

O'Toole was less familiar with the workings of the railway, and was watching the trains going into the mouth of a tunnel. He was enthralled. A fellow saw him staring and asked, "What's so interesting down there?"

O'Toole said, "'Tis marvellous . . . They go plumb in the hole every time."

McGinty was retiring and had bought a plot of ground ready to build a bungalow. His friend Riley said, "Why d'ye not buy one of those railway carriages they're selling? Ye'd have a ready-made bungalow."

So McGinty bought one. Some time afterwards, he was sitting in a deck chair, in the rain, puffing contentedly at his pipe. Riley happened along and said, "Are ye crazy sitting there in the rain?" McGinty said, "No, 'tis very awkward ye see...I bought a non-smoker."

Did you hear about how Paddy ripped off the railway? He bought a return ticket and never came back.

A surgeon and an architect, both English, were joined by an Irish politician and all fell to arguing as to whose profession was the oldest.

Said the surgeon, "Eve was made from Adam's rib, and that surely was a surgical operation."

"Maybe," said the architect, "but prior to that, order was created out of chaos and that was an architectural job."

"Shure now," interrupted the politician, "but somebody created the chaos first."

A Dublin newspaper office received an unusual call.

"We have seen," said a feminine voice, "a number of references in the press to the law of supply and demand. Could you kindly inform us what this law is and when it was passed?"

An Irish lawyer, having occasion to go to dinner, left these directions written and put in the keyhole of his chamber door:

"I am gone to the *Elephant and Castle*, where you shall find me. If you can't read this note, carry it next door and my neighbour will read it for you."

A woman telephoned an airline office in Dublin and asked, "How long does it take to fly to London?"

The clerk said, "Just a minute."

"Thank you," the woman said as she hung up.

That same Irishwoman's nephew was the one who moved his house two feet forward, to take up the slack in his clothesline.

These two Irishmen were even worse. One said, "Where was ye when I met ye on the bridge, Mick?"

The other one said, "I didn't notice ye as ye passed...Then when I looked round, ye'd gone."

The Irish driving student was being put through his paces by the licensing officer. When asked what an unbroken yellow line meant he replied: "No parking at all!" He was then asked what two unbroken yellow lines meant. "No parking at all at all" was the speedy reply.

Paddy and Mick were driving a big combine harvester right down the middle of the road. A visitor to Ireland came round the bend in a car, doing about fifty miles an hour, and had to brake sharply. He finished up doing two complete somersaults and landed upside down in a field.

Paddy turned to Mick and said, "Did ye see that?"

Mick said, "Oi shure did . . . we just got out of that field in time, Pat."

"**S**ean," said Mick, "did you know we only use one third of our brains?"

"No," said Sean. "What happens to the other third?"

Mick was on his way to the market, with a donkey he was going to sell. As he was trudging along the road, a friend met him and said, "Why de ye not take it on the train? It'll save ye the long walk."

Mick did this, and as the train came in, he started to drag the donkey into the carriage with him. This was too much, even for the Irish porter. The porter said, "Ye can't do that. Put it at the back."

Mick didn't know that the porter meant the guard's van. He tied the donkey to the buffers at the back of the train.

The train was going at about fifty miles an hour, and Mick, looking out of the window, said, "I guess Dennis is picking his feet up now."

But when the train arrived at the station, there was no sign of Dennis.

Mick went along to the train driver, and said, "Did ye notice a donkey pass ye?"

Among his neighbours Rafferty is known as a man of great sagacity. They tell the story of the day he was trying to get a donkey under a bridge. The bridge was too low. The donkey's ears wouldn't go under. So Rafferty started to chisel some of the brickwork away from the ceiling of the bridge.

Murphy arrived and said, "Wouldn't it be easier to dig a foot away out of the ground?"

Rafferty said, "Will ye use yer brains? 'Tis his ears that are the trouble."

Then there was Murphy who was given two weeks to live.

He decided to take one week in July and the other in September.

Have you heard the one about the Irishman who thought manual labour was a Spanish tennis star?

An American, an Englishman and an Irishman were travelling through the desert when their jeep broke down. They decided to walk to the nearest settlement.

The American said, "I'll take the water so we have something to drink."

The Englishman said, "And I'll take the food so we have something to eat."

The Irishman said, "Oi'll get the door off the jeep so when it gets too hot we can wind down the window."

What's the difference between a ham sandwich and an Irishman?

A ham sandwich is only half an inch thick.

And what's the difference between 100 ham sandwiches and an Irishman?

Nothing.

Pat wanted to borrow money from Mike, who happened to have a small boy with him at the time.

"'Tis a fine kid you have there, Mike," said Pat. "A magnificent head and noble features. Could you loan me ten?"

"I could not," replied Mike. "'Tis me wife's child by her first husband."

"**D**ada," said Sean's young son, "will you help me blow up balloons for my party?"

"Certainly not," said Sean. "You're much too young to play with explosives."

What are the best ten years of an Irishman's life? Third grade.

And then there was the Irish Setter, sitting in the corner gnawing on a bone.
When he stood up he only had three legs.

Pat was dawdling along on his way to work, looking half asleep. Mike overtook him and slapped him on the back.

"What's wrong wid ye this fine mornin'?" he cried. "It's half asleep you're looking."

Pat turned a bleary eye on his friend. "And it's half asleep I'm feelin'," he said. "Wasn't I up half the night?"

"What was the trouble?"

"It was the cat," replied Pat. "Wasn't I sittin' there till gone two, waiting for her to come in so I could put her out for the night?"

Then there's the one about the Irish jellyfish — it set.

Why do Irish dogs have flat noses? Because they chase parked cars.

Kelly had two horses he could never tell apart. It caused him lots of trouble until one day he discovered that the black horse was two hands taller than the white one.

An Irishman was walking down the street with a sack over his shoulder when a friend approached.

"What have you got in the sack, Mick?"

"Chickens, Pat, and I'll tell you what — if you can guess how many I've got, I'll give you both of them."

Pat answered: "Three?"

What's the definition of a dope ring?
    Six Irishmen in a circle.

Two Irishmen met and one said to the other, "Have ye seen Mulligan lately, Pat?"

Pat said, "Well, I have, and I haven't."

His friend said, "And what d'ye mean by that?"

Pat said, "It's like this, ye see . . . I saw a chap who I thought was Mulligan, and he saw a chap that he thought was me. And when we got up to one another . . . it was neither of us."

It was general questions time on "Top of the World" quiz and the compere first asked the Australian:

"Complete this line of a song and spell your answer — Old MacDonald had a..."

The Australian answered quickly: "Station — STATION."

Next it was the American who was asked the same question:

"Old MacDonald had a..."

"Ranch," replied the American, "RANCH."

Finally the Irishman was asked the same question:

"Old MacDonald had a..."

"Farm," the Irishman replied.

"Correct," said the compere. "Now spell the word farm."

The Irishman hesitated. "EIEIO."

Then there was the Irishman on "Mastermind".

He was sitting in the hot seat waiting for his first question.

"What's your name and occupation?" the compere asked.

"Pass," he responded.

How does an Irish firing squad line up? In a circle. Or...

How does an Irish firing squad line up? One behind the other.

An American, an Englishman and an Irishman were all facing a firing squad. The men in the squad were loading their guns and this gave the American time to talk to the other two.

"Listen, you two, one at a time we will think of a means of distraction and when they are turning their backs, the one that creates it runs over the hill. I'll go first and show you," he said.

The squad lined up and took aim. Quickly the American shouted, "Tornado!"

The squad as a man turned around to look and the American ran over the hill.

Then it was the Englishman's turn. As the squad aimed, he yelled out, "Flash flood!"

At this also, the squad turned expecting to see a large wave of water. But there was nothing and when they turned back the Englishman had vanished also.

Now it was the Irishman's turn. As the squad aimed the Irishman, thinking quickly, yelled out, "Fire!"

Paddy was in the cavalry and had been given a very spirited horse to ride. He got into such a tangle that the horse got its hoof caught up in the stirrup iron.

Paddy looked down, and saw this.

"Be jabbers," he said, "if ye're getting up here, I'm getting off."

We've all heard the disaster stories that came in the wake of the American embassy siege in Iran, but the details of yet another one are only now becoming generally known.

The highly trained Irish back-up team *did* manage to get through all right, but misread their instructions, shot their way into the Teheran zoo and released 57 ostriches.

One of the simplest military devices is the Irish mine detector. You put your hands over your ears and with one outstretched foot sort of tap the ground in front of you...

An Irishman was trying to enlist in the army. He said he was 41 whereas the age limit was 38. But the recruiting sergeant thought the Irishman would make a good soldier and told him to go out and think about the age matter and return. In an hour the Irishman was back.

"Well, how old are you now?" asked the sergeant.

"Sure, it's 38 Oi am; it's me old mither who is 41."

Heard the latest innovation in Irish submarines? Screen windows to keep the fish out.

How do you sink an Irish submarine?
Knock on the hatch.

How do you drown 50 Irishmen?
Get them to push start a submarine.

The two Irish sailors were great pals. One was a gunner, and the other one was a cook. Mike, the cook, was also very keen to become a gunner and was always on deck, asking Pat all about the gun.

One day Mike said, "Pat, let me fire just one shot."

Pat said, "'Tis too dangerous. The skipper would hear it."

Mike said, "He won't hear it if I hold me bucket over the muzzle."

Mike won, and Pat let him load the gun. Mike held the bucket over the muzzle and the shot was fired. Away went the bucket, with Mike hanging on to it!

The noise aroused the whole crew, and the skipper stormed up and said, "Who the hell fired it?"

Pat said, "'Twas Mike Murphy, sor!"

The skipper said, "Where is he?"

Pat said, "He's away to get a bucket of water, sor . . . But if he gets back as fast as he went, he's due back any second."

Did you hear about the Irishman who was given a pair of water-skis? He spent the rest of his life looking for a sloping lake. Eventually he was killed trying to slalom down a waterfall.

The matron was inquiring about the young man in ward ten. He was swathed in bandages and had obviously had a nasty accident. She was told he was a member of the British bobsleigh team.

"My goodness, you must have had a dreadful spill," she said. "What happened?"

"We met the Irish team coming up!"

Did you hear about the Irish marksman who shot an arrow into the air and missed?

His brother was Ireland's champion parachutist. He jumped out of a plane and missed the earth.

Racehorse doping is not unknown in Ireland. One day, the Clerk of the Course spotted a trainer giving something to a horse just before the start of a race. He went over and said, "Doping?" The trainer said, "Indeed not, Sor. 'Tis just lump sugar. Look, I'll take a bit meself...see?"

The Clerk of the Course said, "Sorry, but we have to be careful. As a matter of fact, I like a bit of sugar meself."

So the trainer gave him a piece.

When the Clerk of the Course disappeared, the trainer rushed over to the jockey and said, "Don't forget the drill. Hold him in till the last four furlongs. Don't worry if anything passes ye. It'll be me or the Clerk of the Course."

"**P**addy, Oi missed the soccer. What was the score?"

"Shure 'twas a great game they played Mick," said Paddy. "The score was nil all."

"And what was it at half time?"

"Oi don't know Mick. Oi was only there for the second half."

Did you hear about the Irish grand prix driver? He made 100 pit stops — four for fuel and the other 96 for directions.

Almost unbelievably there was an Irish Evel Knievel. He died trying to jump over 23 motorbikes in a bus.

Sir Thomas Lipton was Irish and he was also a very keen yacht racing enthusiast. He tried hard to win the world's greatest yacht race, but he never did. He managed second place several times, but the big prize always eluded him. His yachts were all named Shamrock and the Irish were always rooting for him.

It was on one of these hard luck occasions that Paddy said, "He's failed again."

His English friend said, "You know what it is, Pat? They put something in the water."

"I've always had me suspicions," said Pat. "What do they put in?"

His friend said, as he made a quick getaway, "The other yachts."

Paddy: "Did yez mark the place where the fishing was so good?"

Mick: "Yes, Oi put an 'x' on the side of the boat."

Paddy: "Shure! What if we should take the wrong boat next time?"

Sean was fishing and it started to rain. So he went under the bridge for shelter.

His pal saw him and said, "Are ye afraid of a few spots of rain, Sean?"

Sean said, "I'm not...the fish come here for shelter."

Paddy was out in a boat with his friend McGinty, and the boat sprang a leak at one end. Paddy made a hole at the other end, saying, "'Tis all right, so — this'll let it out."

Did you hear about the Irish waterpolo team? They drowned four horses during the first chukka.

Paddy was trapped in a bog and seemed a goner when Big Mick O'Reilly walked by.

"Help," Paddy shouted, "Oi'm sinking."

"Don't worry," assured Mick, "Oi'm the strongest man in Ireland and Oi'll pull you out."

Mick leaned over and grabbed Paddy's hand and pulled and pulled to no avail. After two more unsuccessful attempts Mick said to Paddy, "Oi'm the strongest man in Ireland, and if Oi can't pull you out Oi'll have to get some help."

Just as Mick was about to leave, Paddy shouted "Mick, Mick, do you think it will help if Oi take my feet out of the stirrups?"

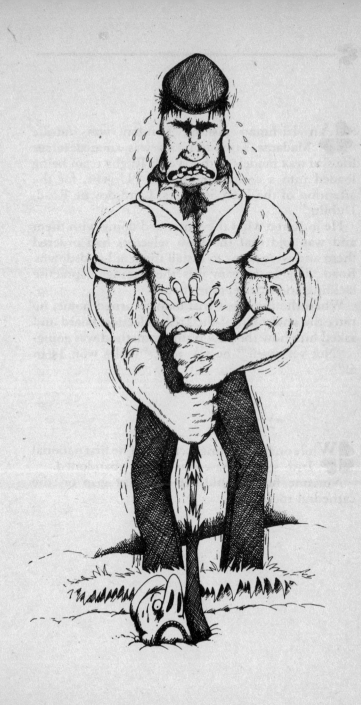

❦ An Irishman visiting London was outside
Madame Tussaud's and was amazed to see
life-size wax models of the Welsh Rugby team being
loaded into a container marked "Urgent, for the
attention of the Irish Selectors, Landsdowne Road,
Dublin."

He inquired what they intended doing with them
and was told that the Irish selectors had ordered
them and were going to install them at Landsdowne
Road. The Irish team was then going to practise
tackling and sidestepping them.

When the intrigued Irishman returned home, he
rang the chairman of the Irish selection board and
asked him how the new training method was going.

"Not very well," he was told. "Wales won 14 to
6!"

❦ While on the sporting scene . . . The first national
Irish steeplechase was finally abandoned.

Not one horse could get a decent grip on the
cathedral roof.

It is a well-known fact that many Irish Roman Catholic priests are enthusiasts of horse racing, and the number of them who frequent the festival meetings held in Britain has to be seen to be believed. Betting on horses is one of their first loves.

Just before the final race at the four-day Ascot meeting, Father Murphy and Father O'Flanagan were seen deep in conversation at the side of the parade ring. And, standing quite close to them, was the race commentator who was busily studying the colours of the jockeys just about to mount their horses. However, he overheard what the two priests were saying to each other:

Father Murphy: "Well Father O'Flanagan, I've had a terrible meeting, hardly backing a winner at all during all of the four days. Therefore I've got to back the winner of this race, the 'Getting Out' Stakes. I don't know what my parishioners will say if I don't take something home."

Father O'Flanagan: "I too am in that position, Father Murphy, and I'm equally anxious to back the winner of this meeting's last race."

Father Murphy: "Having a good look at the runners here, as well as studying their past form, I honestly think Lester Piggott will win this race. I'm therefore going to risk all my remainder on him."

Father O'Flanagan: "I'm of the same mind as you Father, and I too am going to wager my last bit of money on Lester. Before doing so, though, I'm going to offer a little prayer and trust the Almighty will answer it." So without more ado, off came his black hat, and he turned his eyes towards the heavens. "Holy Father, Heavenly Grace, may Lester Piggott win this race."

Whereupon Father Murphy pulled off his hat too. "I too am going to offer a little prayer and ask the

Almighty for a little help." So he too turned his eyes towards the heavens. "Holy Father up in Heaven, and may his winner be 100 to 7."

The race commentator, who could hear all this, made his way up to the commentator's box. The horses 'came under starter's orders', closely followed by 'They're off', and the race commentator began:

"This is the voice of the Holy Ghost; Lester Piggott's been left at the post."

 Paddy was showing an American some Irish marrows, and the American said they had gherkins as big as the marrows.

Then Paddy showed him some large cabbages. The American said they had brussels sprouts as big and added that an average American cabbage would be about three feet in diameter.

Eventually, the American pointed to some gasometers and said, "We haven't anything like them in the States. What are they?"

Paddy said, "They're Oirish saucepans. We cook American cabbages in them."

It was Paddy's brother who visited America and while there went into a pizza parlour. When his pizza was ready the man behind the counter asked whether he wanted it cut into four pieces or six.

"Better make it four," said Paddy's brother. "Oi don't think Oi could eat six."

A boasting American said to O'Connor, "Back home in the States we can erect a block of skyscrapers in about two weeks."

O'Connor was ready for him. He said, "We can beat that. I was on my way to work the other day and they'd started building a row of cottages. When I was on my way home, they were putting the bailiffs in. The tenants were behind with their rents."

Did you hear about the Irish godfather who kept making offers he couldn't remember?

The Irish have hit a snag in their effort to join the space race. They've developed a rocket, but they can't find a bottle big enough to hold the stick.

The Irishman was telling an American about Ireland's plan to send a manned rocket to the sun.

"But you can't do that," said the American, "the rocket will burn up."

"It's okay," said the Irishman, "we're sending it up at night."

On his hundredth birthday a reluctant Irish potato grower, being interviewed by a reporter from the city, was asked: "I suppose you've seen a great many changes in your time?"

"Yes," replied the centenarian, "and I've been agin' 'em *all!*"

A famous linguist who was visiting Ireland was moved to ask an Irish colleague whether there was any word in the Irish language that had the same meaning as the Spanish mañana.

The Irishman pondered well before replying. "Shure," he said, "we've about two or three that come close. But none of them have the same sense of urgency."

" Sean, do you understand French?" "Yis, if it's shpoke in Oirish."

An Englishman, a Welshman and a Scotsman were left legacies by a friend on condition that each should put £5 in his coffin.

The Englishman put in a £5 note. The Welshman also put in £5 which he had borrowed from the Englishman.

The Scotsman took out the two £5 notes and put in a cheque for £15 payable to bearer.

Three days later he was astonished to learn that the cheque had been presented and cashed. The undertaker was an Irishman.

The origin of the bagpipes was being discussed and the representatives of different nations were eagerly disclaiming responsibility for the instrument.

Finally an Irishman said, "Well, I'll tell you the truth about it. The Irish invented them and sold them to the Scots as a joke; and the Scots haven't seen the joke yet!"

An Irishman was digging a hole when his friend approached.

"What are you doing?" inquired the friend.

"I'm digging a hole to bury my dog," replied the intrepid excavator.

"Well, what are these other three holes for?" persisted the friend.

The Irishman explained: "They were going to be to bury the dog in but they weren't big enough."

The bus was crowded when an old Irishwoman got on, and had to stand. A polite lad stood up and asked, "Would you like my seat for a while?"

"No," she said, "I daren't sit down, I'm in a hurry."

How do you burn an Irishman's ear?
    Ring him up while he's ironing.
How did the Irishman burn his other ear?
He had to ring the doctor.

Here's an Irish telephone conversation:
    "Is that Dublin double two, double three, double two?"
    "No. This is Dublin two two, three three, two two."
    "Oh. Wrong number. Sorry to disturb ye."
    "Don't be worrying. Shure the phone was ringing and I had to answer it anyway."

Murphy was selling his house, and put the matter in an agent's hands. The agent wrote his advertisement for the house and it made wonderful reading.
    After Murphy read it, he turned to the agent and said, "Have I got all ye say there?"
    The agent said, "Certainly ye have...Why?"
    Murphy said, "Cancel the sale...'tis too good to part with."

What do you do if an Irishman throws a pin at you?

Run. He's probably got a grenade in his mouth.

What do you do if an Irishman throws a grenade at you?

Pull the pin out and throw it back.

The I.R.A. man, killed in a bomb blast, is met by St Peter at the Pearly Gates.

"Oi'm O'Hara of the Belfast branch," says he.

"Well, you can't come in here," says St Peter. "We don't want all that trouble in heaven."

"Oi don't want to come in," says O'Hara. "You've got ten minutes to clear the place."

Surely everyone is by now well acquainted with the Irishman who was sent to London to blow up a bus and burnt his lips on the exhaust pipe.

Two Irishmen are driving to a pub with a bomb in the back and evil plans in their minds.

One turns to the other and says, "What if the bomb goes off before we get there?"

The other replies, "Don't worry, I've got a spare in the boot."

What's the fastest game in the world?
Pass the parcel in an Irish pub.

Paddy and Mick were passing a bombed out pub where the above game had been in progress only minutes before. As they went by, a head rolled out of the smouldering ruins and onto the pavement before them. Paddy stooped, picked it up and held it up for Mick to see.

"Shure now Mick, isn't this Sean Murphy?"

"No Paddy, no it couldn't be. It's an amazin' resemblance but Murphy was shorter than that."

Mick had formed a dance band, and they were working their very first engagement at the village hall. Mick was very excited about it all, and said to the trombone player, "Paddy . . . go outside and listen to what it sounds like, will yer?"

The trombonist went out and after a while came back and said, "'Tis terrific . . . you should hear it."

And the whole band went outside to listen . . .

Did you hear about the Irishman who wanted to tap dance?
He broke his ankle when he fell off the sink.

The reason Irishmen usually go about in groups of three is that one can usually read, one can usually write, and the third likes to hang around with intellectuals.

A visitor to a little hamlet in Ireland commented, "What a quiet little place."

The constable said, "'Tis quiet, to be sure. We haven't buried a living soul for years."

There must be thousands of Patrick Murphys around the world. This particular one had been hitting the bottle a bit. He wandered into a graveyard and slept it off on one of the graves.

When he came to, he looked up and read the inscription on the tombstone. It said, "Here lies the body of Patrick Murphy."

He said, "'Tis me all right. But, divil a bit — I don't remember the first thing about the funeral."

An English gent was coming home late one night when a masked man popped out of an alley and said, "This is a hold-up. Put your hands up, or else!"

"Or else what?" the gent asked testily.

"Don't be gettin' me confused," the masked man begged, hoarsely. "This is me first job."

An Irishman was held up by a bandit with the usual demand: "Your money or your life!"

"Take my life," said the Irishman. "Oi'll be after saving me money for me old age."

An Irish delinquent was in court for non-payment of maintenance to his previous wife. The magistrate weighed the case up, and said, "I've decided to increase this allowance, and give your wife £5 per week."

Pat said, "Ye're a gintleman Sor . . . Oi might send her a few bob meself too."

♣ Paddy and Sean decided to rob a London bank, but were afraid their accents would give them away. They thought about handing over a hold-up note, but neither could write. Finally they employed an elocutionist.

On the big day they entered the bank, pointed their sawn-off shotguns at the teller and said: "Ah say old chap, give us the money or we'll blow your head off."

The teller looked up calmly. "You're Irish, aren't you?"

"But how did you know?" said Paddy. "Our accents were perfect."

"Yeah," said the teller, "but you've sawn your shotguns off at the wrong end."

♣ How can you pick the Irish pirate?
He's the one with patches over both eyes.

♣ O'Hagan had joined the Metropolitan Police Force. He was being shown his beat by the sergeant.

After a while, the sergeant said, "This is the end of your beat...that red light over there."

O'Hagan was missing for a fortnight, and when he reported back the sergeant asked, "Where the hell have you been?"

"Manchester and back," said O'Hagan. "That red light was on the back of a lorry."

The Irish policeman pulled up beside Paddy who was driving a brand-new Mercedes.

"Pull over and out ye get," he roared. Paddy obliged.

"Now," said the cop, "Oi don't believe for a minute that yez own this car and Oi'm going to make yez tell me who does." So saying he drew a chalk circle on the ground.

"Stand inside that and stay there. Now if yez don't tell me who owns this Oi'm goin' to smash the dashboard." Paddy made no reply, so the cop turned and smashed all the glass on the dashboard meters. He turned back to find Paddy smiling.

Furious, he shouted, "Shure now, Oi'm not joking. Tell me who owns the car or Oi'll rip the seats to pieces."

Paddy stood in the circle and said nothing, so the cop set to work and ripped the leather upholstery to shreds. Again he turned back to Paddy who was by now grinning broadly.

"A joke, yez think it's a joke, do yez?" roared the cop. "For the last time, man, tell me who owns the car or Oi'll set fire to it." But Paddy stood his ground and said nothing. So the cop made good his word. He threw petrol all over the gleaming Mercedes and set fire to it. As the flames engulfed the once magnificent motorcar he turned to find Paddy doubled up with laughter.

"Ye great lummox," roared the cop. "Now Oi know it's not yer car. Shure yez wouldn't be laughing if 'twas."

"Oi'm not laughing at that," Paddy chokes out, the tears of laughter rolling down his cheeks, "it's just that every time yez turned yer back Oi jumped out of the circle!"

The judge asked the accused Irishman if there was anyone in court who could vouch for his good character.

"Yes, Yer Honour," said the Irishman, "there's the sheriff."

"Why, Your Honour," said the sheriff, "I don't even know the man."

"Observe, Yer Honour," said the Irishman triumphantly, "observe that Oi've lived in the country for over twelve years an' the sheriff doesn't know me yit! Ain't that a character for ye?"

Mick was walking down the street when suddenly two men pulled him into an alley. Mick put up a terrific fight, but the thugs succeeded in getting him pinned down, and robbed him. When they found only thirty pence, one of the men said, angrily:

"You mean to say you put up that fierce fight for a measly thirty pence?"

Mick replied: "Oh, no! Oi thought yez were after the five hundred pounds Oi have hidden in my shoe."

♣ Mick had decided to join the police force and went along for the entrance examination.

The examining sergeant, realising that the prospective recruit was an Irishman, decided to ask him a simple question. "Who killed Jesus Christ?" he asked.

Mick looked worried and said nothing, so the sergeant told him not to worry and that he could have some time to think about it.

Mick was on his way home when he met Paddy.

"Well," said Paddy, "are you a policeman yet?"

"Not only that," says Mick, "but I'm on my first case."

♣ The police pulled Paddy in for suspected rape. They put him in a line-up with ten other fellas and the accusing woman was brought in.

Paddy jumped forward. "That's her," he screamed. "That's her, I'd recognise her anywhere."

♣ Did you hear the one about the Irish rapist? He tied the girl's legs together so she couldn't run away.

Grow your own dope. Plant an Irishman.

"Well, Mrs O'Connor, so you want a divorce?" the solicitor questioned his client. "Tell me about it. Do you have a grudge?"

"Oh no," replied Mrs O'Connor. "Shure now, we have a carport."

The solicitor tried again. "Well does the man beat you up?" he inquired.

"No, no," said Mrs O'Connor looking puzzled. "Oi'm always first out of bed."

Still hopeful, the solicitor tried again. "Well does he go in for unnatural connubial practices?"

"Shure now, he plays the flute but I don't think he knows anything about the connubial."

Now desperate, the solicitor pushed on. "What I'm trying to find out are what grounds you have?"

"Bless ye, sor. We live in a flat — not even a window box, let alone grounds."

"Mrs O'Connor," said the solicitor in some exasperation, "to get a divorce you need a reason that the court can consider. What is the reason for you seeking this divorce?"

"Ah well now," said the lady. "Shure it's because the man can't hold an intelligent conversation."